A-LEVEL CHEMISTRY

FLASH NOTES

AQA Year 1 and AS

New Syllabus 2015

Dr C.

GW00482116

Condensed Revision Notes (Flashcards) for a
Successful Exam Preparation

Designed to Facilitate Memorization

www.alevelchemistryrevision.co.uk

Text copyright © 2015 Dr. Christoph Boes

Cover Image copyright © Pedro Antonio Salaverría Calahorra
Dreamstime.com (Image ID: 12739630)
http://www.dreamstime.com/pedro2009_info

All other Images copyright © 2015 Dr. Christoph Boes

Self-published 2015

ISBN-13: 978-0-9957060-1-9

How to use these notes

Revision notes (revision cards) are an effective and successful way to prepare for exams. They contain the necessary exam knowledge in a condensed, easy to memorize form. These notes are designed for the final stage of revision and require a thorough understanding of the topics. If this understanding is lacking then help from a professional tutor and additional studies of text books or revision guides is suggested.

These revision notes are organized in different chapters according to the new 2015 AQA Year 1 & AS syllabus. Each chapter contains individual revision cards covering all the necessary topics. Everything in *italic* is optional knowledge, aimed at students who want to excel or want to continue to year 2. **Bold** represents important keywords or key definitions. 'Data sheet' indicates information which will be provided on the data sheet during the exam and does not need to be memorized. Important information and exam-specific tips are highlighted in yellow or grey.

How to memorize: The revision cards are introduced by their titles and keywords on a separate page. After reading the title you should try to write down the content of the card without looking at the next page. The keywords give you hints about the content. Write down everything you remember, even if you are not sure. Then check if your answers are correct; if not, rewrite the incorrect ones.

At the beginning, when you are still unfamiliar with the cards, it might help to read them a few times first. If they contain a lot of content, you can cover the revision card with a piece of paper and slowly reveal the header and sub content. While you uncover it try to remember what is written in the covered part, e.g. the definition for a term you just uncovered. This uncovering technique is for the early stages, later you should be able to write down the whole content after just reading the header. If this is the case, move to the next card. If not, bookmark the card and memorize it repeatedly. Do at least three to four sessions per week until you know all the cards in one chapter word-perfectly. Then move on to the next section. Generally it is better to do shorter sessions more often than longer sessions less frequently.

An even better memorization option is to ask somebody to check your knowledge by reading the header aloud and comparing your answer to the content. Alternatively, get together in learning groups and support each other. Make it a game to check your knowledge by creating questions and compete as groups like in a pub quiz. Discuss questions which you don't understand; your friend might know the answers or ask your teacher or tutor. More tips about memorization techniques and how to prepare for exams can be found on my website: http://www.alevelchemistryrevision.co.uk

Disclaimer: Due to the changing nature of mark schemes it cannot be guaranteed that answers according to these notes will give you full marks. These notes constitute only a part of a full revision program, alongside other methods like practising past papers. They have been created with great care; however, errors or omissions cannot be excluded.

Contents

Unit 1 – Physical Chemistry

1.1 Atomic Structure

Basic Definitions

Atom; Element; Isotopes; Atomic number; Mass number; Ion; Relative atomic mass with equation; Relative isotopic mass; Molar mass; Relative molecular mass

Basic Definitions

Atom: smallest unit of an element
-> consist of electrons organized in orbitals/shells and a nucleus made from protons and neutrons

Subatomic Particle	Relative mass	Charge
Proton	1	+1
Neutron	1	0
Electron	1/2000	-1

Element: same kind of atoms (same atomic number)

Isotopes: atoms with same number of protons but different number of neutrons
(same element: same atomic number but different mass number)

Atomic number: number of protons

Mass number: protons + neutrons

Ion: charged particle
positive -> **cation**
negative -> **anion**
=> formed when an atom gains or loses electrons to get a full outer shell

Relative Atomic mass A_r
Is the average (weighted) mass of an element's isotopes relative to 1/12 the mass of a ^{12}C atom [no unit]

$$A_r = \frac{(a\% \times A_1) + (b\% \times A_2)}{100}$$

a%: percentage of Isotope 1
b%: percentage of Isotope 2
A_1: Relative Isotopic mass of Isotope 1
A_2: Relative Isotopic mass of Isotope 2

=> A_r and **Relative Isotopic Abundance** can be worked out from a Mass Spectrum (a%, b% from y-axis of each peak) -> see revision card 'Mass Spectrometry'

Relative isotopic mass
Is the mass of an atom of an isotope relative to 1/12 the mass of a ^{12}C atom [no unit]

Molar mass M
Mass of one mole of a substance [g mol^{-1}]

Relative molecular Mass M_r (relative formula mass)
of a compound is the sum of the relative atomic masses of all its atoms [no unit]

Electron Configuration

*Definition for orbital; Three rules; Meaning of the numbers &
letters; Box diagram; Shapes of orbitals; Table of subshells;
Number of electrons per shell*

Electron Configuration

Orbitals
Definition: Region of space in which electrons are most likely to be found; one orbital contains maximum two electrons, which must have opposite spins.
- Orbitals of the same subshell are filled individually first
- 4s get filled and emptied before 3d (see revision card 'transition metals')
- For cations take off electrons, for anions add electrons according to charge

N: $1s^2\,2s^2\,\mathbf{2p^3}$ [He] $2s^2\,2p^3$

         2: shell
         p: subshell *(letters from spectral lines "sharp", "principal"...)*
           ^{3}: number of electrons (in subshell)

Box diagram:

Electronic configuration of N

Shapes of orbitals:
s-orbital: p-orbital:

Sphere   Dumbbell

Subshells	Orbitals	Electrons
s	1	2
p	3	6
d	5	10
f	7	14

Number of electrons per shell (n): $\mathbf{2n^2}$

1.2 Amount of Substance

Mole & Molar Gas Volume

Mole: Definition, two equations;
Equation for molar gas volume; Converting cm^3 into dm^3; Ideal
gas equation

Mole

1 mole = 6.02×10^{23} (Avogadro's number N_A -> data sheet)

Definition: number of atoms in 12 g of ^{12}C

$$n = \frac{m}{M_r}$$

n: number of moles [moles]
m: mass [g]
M_r: molar mass [g/mol]
[ ]: units

$$N = n \times N_A$$

N: number of particles [no unit]
N_A: Avogadro's number 6.02×10^{23} [mol^{-1}]

Molar Gas Volume

Volume of **1 mole** of any **gas** = $24 \, dm^3$ (data sheet) at **standard conditions** (**298° K/25° C, 100 kPa**)

$$V_x = n \times 24 \, dm^3 \, mol^{-1}$$

V_x: unknown volume [dm^3]
n: number of moles [moles]

Converting cm^3 into dm^3:

$$x \, cm^3 = \frac{x}{1000} \, dm^3$$

Ideal gas equation:

$$pV = nRT$$

p: pressure **[Pa]**
V: volume **[m^3]**
R: 8.31 J K^{-1} mol^{-1} (gas constant -> data sheet)
T: temperature **[K]**   (0° C = 273° K)

-> make sure you are using correct SI units - see [ ]

Empirical and Molecular Formulae

Definitions; Empirical formula from grams; Empirical Formula from percentages; Molecular formulae from empirical formulae and molecular mass; Example Calculation

Empirical and Molecular Formulae

Molecular formula: Actual number of atoms in a molecule, e.g. Ethene C_2H_4
=> closer to reality; generally used in equations.

Empirical formula: Smallest whole number ratio of atoms in a compound; CH_2
=> Empirical formula is used when trying to find out the molecular formula of an unknown organic compound by burning it (elemental analysis)

- For Salts: chemical formula is identical with empirical formula
- For Molecules: molecular formula is a multiple of empirical formula

Work out empirical formulae from grams (burning hydrocarbon):
- Use n=m/M to calculate moles of each element; take mole ratios into account, e.g. H in H_2O $2 : 1$
- Divide by smallest mole number to get ratio (empirical formula)

How to work out empirical formulae from percentages:
- Set 100 % as 100 g, then same as above

Work out molecular formulae from empirical formulae and molecular mass
- Divide molecular M_r by empirical M_r to get factor
- Multiply empirical formula with factor to get molecular formula

Example calculation

When an unknown hydrocarbon with M_r = 70 g/mol is burnt in excess oxygen, we get **6.6 g** of **CO_2** and **2.7 g** of **H_2O** (elemental analysis).
What is the empirical and molecular formula of this compound?

Calculate empirical formula first
Moles CO_2:
n = **6.6 g**/44 g/mol = 0.15 mol (1 mole C in 1 mole CO_2 -> factor 1)
=> Moles C: n = 0.15 mol

Moles H_2O:
n = 2.7 g/18 g/mol = 0.15 mol (2 mole H in 1 mole H_2O -> factor 2)
=> Moles H: n = 2 x 0.15 mol = 0.3 mol

Divide by smallest mole number:
C 0.15/0.15 = 1, **H** 0.3/0.15 = 2
Ratio   **C : H   1 : 2**
Empirical formula: C_1H_2 => CH_2

Calculate Molecular formula from Mr and empirical formula
Unknown hydrocarbon   **M_r = 70 g/mol**
Empirical molar mass CH_2 M_r = 14 g/mol
Factor: 70 g/mol / 14 g/mol = 5
Molecular formula: 5 x **CH_2** => **C_5H_{10}**
=> Unknown Hydrocarbon was Pentene

Water of Crystallisation

Terms; Characteristics; Example Calculation

Water of crystallisation

Terms

Anhydrous salt -> no water
Hydrated salt -> water incorporated in lattice

- Water of crystallisation is expressed with dot and mole number in chemical formula
  -> **water is included in molar mass M_r** and belongs to the compound.
  -> the number of moles H_2O per mole salt is written in the formula:
  $Na_2CO_3\cdot\mathbf{10H_2O}$ $M_r = 286$ g/mol ($2x23 + 12 + 3x16 + \mathbf{10x18}$)
- when heated hydrated salts lose water of crystallisation and become lighter (anhydrous)
- difference in mass is due to the water lost and can be used to calculate the number of moles of water of crystallisation in the chemical formula (**X**):
  -> Calculate moles H_2O and moles anhydrous salt by using $n = m/M$
  -> Divide moles of H_2O by moles of anhydrous salt to get **X**
  -> Similar to calculating empirical formulas

Example Calculation

When **6.42 g** of **hydrated magnesium sulphate**, $MgSO_4\cdot\mathbf{X}H_2O$ is heated **3.14 g** of **anhydrous magnesium sulphate** is left. What is the formula of the hydrated salt, e.g. X?

Water lost: 6.42 g – 3.14 g = 3.28 g

Moles H_2O: $n = 3.28$ g$/18$ g mol^{-1} = **0.182 moles**

Moles $MgSO_4$: $n = 3.14$ g$/120$ g mol^{-1} = **0.0261 moles**

X = 0.182 mole / 0.0261 mole = 6.95 = 7

=> $MgSO_4\cdot7H_2O$ *(Epsom salt)*

Mole Equations – Calculate Masses
&
Percentage Yield

Steps; Rounding; Significant figures;
Equation for percentage yield; Converting tonnes in grams;
Reasons for loss

Mole Equations – Calculate Masses

1) Calculate moles for the given compound by using n = m/M
2) Circle or **highlight** mole numbers in front of related compounds (given and **unknown**)
3) Determine mole ratio for unknown compound
4) Get **mole factor** by dividing both mole numbers by the same number (here: 4) so that the given compound becomes 1
5) Multiply moles of given compound with **factor** to get moles of **unknown compound**
6) Calculate mass of unknown compound by using m = n x M
7) Do not round whilst still calculating. Carry as many digits through the calculation as possible (at least 3) until you reach the final answer.
8) Write the answer with the appropriate number of **significant figures**: if the data are given in 3 significant figures then the answer should also be given in 3 significant figures (see below)
9) If the data are given in 2 and 3 significant figures then the answer should be given in 2 significant figures (**always the lowest one**)
10) If the last non-significant figure is 1 - 4 round down, if 5 – 9 round up.
11) $0.001 = 1 \times 10^{-3}$ -> use standard form for scientific calculations

Example

Calculate amount of O_2 (in grams) produced if 3.24 g of iron(III) nitrate is heated

$$4Fe(NO_3)_3 \rightarrow 2Fe_2O_3 + 12NO_2 + 3O_2$$

1) Moles $Fe(NO_3)_3$: n = 3.24 g/ 241.8 g/mol = 0.0134 moles
2) See **mole equation** above
3) Ratio: 3 : 4
4) Factor for O_2: ¾ = 0.75 ($Fe(NO_3)_3$: 4/4 = 1)
5) Moles O_2 : 0.75 x 0.0134 moles = 0.0100 moles
6) Mass O_2: m = n x M = 0.0100 mol x 32 g/mol = 0.322 g

Percentage Yield

percentage yield = __actual yield__   x 100
                        theoretical yield

units of actual/theoretical yield of products: [grams] or [moles]

1 tonne = 1 x 10^6 g

Reasons for loss
- Reaction not complete (clumps instead of powder)
- Loss of product (sticking to vessel, evaporation of liquids)
- By-products
- Impurities of reactants

Atom Economy
&
Concentrations

*Equation for atom economy; Benefits of high atom economy;
Example calculation;
Equations for mole concentrations & mass concentrations;
Converting dm^3 in cm^3;*

Atom Economy

$$\% \text{ atom economy} = \frac{M_r \text{ desired product}}{\Sigma M_r \text{ all products}} \times 100$$

-> 100 % for addition reactions

Benefits of high atom economy
- Environmental and economic benefits
- Avoiding waste
- Reduces separation costs
- High sustainability (less raw material)
- High efficiency

Example calculation

$$(NH_4)_2SO_{4(s)} + 2NaOH_{(aq)} \rightarrow 2NH_{3(g)} + Na_2SO_{4(aq)} + 2H_2O_{(l)}$$

Calculate the percentage atom economy for the production of ammonia

$$\% \text{ atom economy} = \frac{2 \times 17}{2 \times 17 + 142 + 2 \times 18} \times 100$$

$$= 16.0 \%$$

Concentration

Mole concentration:

$$c = \frac{n}{V}$$

n: moles [mol]
V: volume [dm^3]
c: concentration [mol dm^{-3}]

1 dm^3 = 1000 cm^3

Mass concentration:

$$c = \frac{m}{V}$$

m: mass [g]
c: mass concentration [g dm^{-3}]

1.3 Bonding

Ionic and Covalent Compounds and Bonds

Definition for Compound; Names and Characteristics for ionic compounds; Definition ionic bond; Draw lattice; Names and Characteristics for covalent compounds; Definition covalent bond; Definition & symbol for dative covalent bond

Ionic and Covalent Compounds and Bonds

Compound: Atoms of different elements bonded together

Salts - Ionic compounds: Metal/Non metal
- Consist of ions
- 'Dot-and Cross' diagram: square bracket with charge around ion
- Forms lattice with alternating charges (see diagram below)
- Chemical formula gives ratio
- Physical properties:
  - high melting points
  - soluble in water
  - conduct electricity in solution or when molten (ions can move)
- Examples: $NaCl$, $MgCl_2$

Ionic bond: electrostatic attraction between oppositely charged ions

$$
\begin{array}{cccccc}
Na^+ & Cl^- & Na^+ & Cl^- & Na^+ & Cl^- \\
Cl^- & Na^+ & Cl^- & Na^+ & Cl^- & Na^+ \\
Na^+ & Cl^- & Na^+ & Cl^- & Na^+ & Cl^- \\
Cl^- & Na^+ & Cl^- & Na^+ & Cl^- & Na^+
\end{array}
$$

Molecules - Covalent compounds: Non metals
- Collection of atoms
- 'Dot-and Cross' diagram: overlapping circles for bonds
- Different shapes
- Formula tells which atoms are directly connected to each other
- Physical properties:
  - low melting point
  - not soluble in water
  - not conducting electricity
- Examples: CH_4, H_2O

Covalent bond: sharing **a pair** of electrons
-> strong electrostatic attraction between two nuclei (+) and the shared pair of electrons (-)

Dative covalent bond: both electrons of the covalent bond come from **one** atom (arrow instead of dash) e.g. NH_4^+

Shapes of Molecules I

Theory; Shapes for molecules: one central atom with 2, 3, 4 partners; one central atom with 3 partners & 1 lone pair of electrons

Shapes of Molecules

Valence Shell Electron-Pair Repulsion Theory:
- Negative charges of electron pairs in covalent bonds **repel** each other
- Lone pairs of electrons on the central atom repel more (closer to central atom) => smaller bond angle
- **Shape depends on number of charge clouds** (bonds, electron pairs)

One central atom with 2 partners (charge clouds):

=> linear, 180˚, CO_2, $BeCl_2$

One central atom with 3 partners:

F
F
B
120°
F

=> trigonal planar, 120˚, BF_3

One central atom with 4 partners:

H
109.5°
C
H
H
H

H
N
H
H
H
+

=> tetrahedral, 109.5˚, CH_4, NH_4^+ (draw straight-line-bonds next to each other)

One central atom with 3 partners & 1 lone pair of electrons:

N
H
H
H
107°

=> trigonal pyramidal, 107°, NH_3, SO_3^{2-}

One central atom with 2 partners & 2 lone pairs of electrons:

104.5°

=> bent/non-linear, 104.5°, H_2O

Shapes of Molecules II

One central atom with 4 partners and one lone pair of electrons; One central atom with 4 partners & 2 lone pair of electrons; One central atom with 5 partners; One central atom with 6 partners

One central atom with 3 partners and 2 lone pairs of electrons

=> t-shaped, 88°, ClF_3

One central atom with 4 partners and 1 lone pair of electrons:

=> seesaw, 102° & 87°, SF_4

One central atom with 4 partners and 2 lone pairs of electrons:
=> square planar XeF4 -> see A2 revision card 'Stereoisomerism in complexes

One central atom with 5 partners:

=> trigonal bipyramidal, 120°& 90°, PCl_5

One central atom with 6 partners:

=> octahedral, 90°, SF_6

To get other examples: use a different element from the same group as the central atom and keep same partners, e.g. PH_3 for NH_3

--> use the expression 'charge clouds' instead of 'partners' in exam

Electronegativity

Definition; Development across period (one bullet point) and down group (three bullet points)

Electronegativity

Definition: Ability of an atom to attract electrons in a covalent bond

Increases across period:
- more protons

Decreases down group:
- more shells, more distance
- more shielding
- despite more protons

- Fluorine most electronegative element *(then O_2, then Cl_2)*
- Elements closer to F: more electronegative
- *Measured on the Pauling Scale*
- *Large differences in electronegativity result in ionic compounds*
- *Small differences result in covalent compounds*

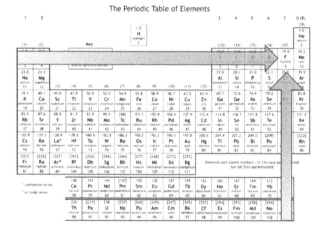

The Periodic Table of Elements

Giant and Simple Covalent Structures
&
Types of Crystal Structures

Definitions of giant covalent structures & allotropes; Allotropes of Carbon; Silica
Simple covalent structures for two elements; Four types of crystal structures

Giant Covalent Structures

- Network of covalently bonded atoms (Macromolecular Structures)
- C, Si => four covalent bonds (Group 4)

Allotropes: pure forms of the same element that differ in structure

Allotropes of carbon:
> **Diamond**: 4 bonds, tetrahedral –> hard, cold, high melting point, not conducting electricity, not soluble
>
> **Graphite**: 3 bonds, trigonal planar, sheets of hexagons -> slippery, lone electrons conduct electricity, strong, lightweight, insoluble

Silica (SiO_2): tetrahedral, hard, crystals, high melting point, insoluble, not conducting electricity => quartz, sand

Simple Covalent Structures (Molecules)

Sulphur: yellow solid, simple molecules like S_8 rings

Phosphorus: white solid, simple molecules like P_4

Types of Crystal Structures

- Ionic (NaCl)
- Metallic (Mg)
- Macromolecular – giant covalent (diamond, graphite)
- Molecular (I_2, ice)

Metallic Bonding

Definition of metallic bonding; Trends of melting point across period (three bullet points) & down group (two bullet points), Characteristics; Diagram;

Metallic Bonding

Definition: Electrostatic attraction between metal **cations** and **delocalized electrons** from the outer shell (**sea of electrons**)
-> high melting points

Across the period higher melting points:
- charges of cations increase: Na^+, Mg^{2+}, Al^{3+}
- more delocalized electrons (negative charges)
- smaller ions (higher charge density)

Down the group lower melting points:
- more shells
- greater distance

Characteristics of metal:
- Electrical & thermal conductors (free moving electrons)
- Malleable & ductile, dense, shiny & soft – only alloys are hard

Giant metallic lattice

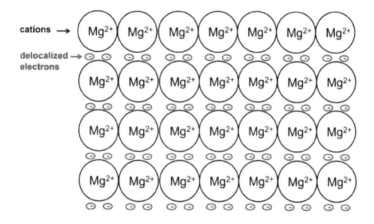

cations →

delocalized → electrons

Intermolecular Forces

Function; Three types; Drawing hydrogen bonds; Anomalous properties of water

Intermolecular Forces

keep molecules together
-> model to explain physical state (melting & boiling points)

The stronger the intermolecular forces the higher the melting/boiling points
-> more energy is required to overcome these forces of attraction

1) Permanent dipole-dipole interactions
Permanent dipoles contain **polar bonds** due to different **electronegativities**
-> shift in electron density

$\delta+$ $\delta-$
H - Cl

δ means slightly (or partially)

Molecules with polar bonds can be permanent dipoles

Polar bonds do not always make polar molecules
Symmetric arrangement where polar bonds cancel each other out => non polar molecule, e.g. CO_2

2) Induced dipole-dipole interactions: London Forces (Van der Waals)
Non-polar molecules contain **non polar bonds** (equal electronegativities: Cl_2)

Temporary/instantaneous dipole
-> Electron cloud moving randomly (uneven distribution); this temporary dipole can induce another dipole
- **depends on number of electrons and surface area (points of contact)**
- weakest intermolecular force

Induced dipole
Permanent dipole or instantaneous dipole can induce dipoles in non-polar molecules, e.g. mixture of HCl and Cl_2

3) Hydrogen Bonds
O, F, N with an H bonded directly to these atoms ($-NH_2$, $-OH$, HF)
- Hydrogen atom flips between two partners (special type of covalent bond)
- 5 – 10 % of the strength of a normal covalent bond, but strongest intermolecular force
- Draw with **dotted line** between H and **lone pair of electrons**:

$\delta+$ $\delta-$ $\delta+$ $\delta-$ $\delta+$ $\delta-$

H— F̈ : ······ H— F̈ : ······ H— F̈ :

Anomalous properties of water
-> high boiling point
-> lower density of ice because of more H-bonds than liquid water

---

1.4 Energetics

Enthalpy Changes – Definitions
&
Bond Enthalpies

Definitions for exothermic/endothermic; Definitions for standard enthalpy change of: reaction, formation, combustion, neutralisation, (atomisation); Definitions for bond dissociation enthalpy & mean bond enthalpy; Equations for ΔH_r; Exothermic/endothermic

Enthalpy Changes - Definitions

Exothermic $-\Delta H_r$ negative: energy released into surroundings
-> heat up

Endothermic $+\Delta H_r$ positive: energy taken from surroundings
-> cool down

ΔH_r : enthalpy change of the reaction [**KJ mol^{-1}**]

Enthalpy change: Heat/energy change in a reaction at constant pressure

Standard enthalpy change $^\Theta$: under standard conditions: 1 atm/100 kPa, 298 K

~ **of reaction** ΔH_r^Θ: is the enthalpy change when the reaction occurs in the **molar quantities** shown in the **chemical equation**, under **standard conditions** in their **standard states**

~ **of formation** ΔH_f^Θ of a compound: is the enthalpy change when **1 mole** of a **compound** is formed from its **elements** in their **standard states** under **standard conditions**
$$2C_{(s)} + 3H_{2(g)} + \tfrac{1}{2}O_{2(g)} \rightarrow C_2H_5OH$$

~ **of combustion** ΔH_c^Θ: is the enthalpy change when **1 mole** of a substance is **completely burned in oxygen** under **standard conditions,** all reactants and products being in their **standard states**

~ **of neutralisation** ΔH_{neut}^Θ: is the enthalpy change when **1 mole of water** is formed from the neutralisation of **(H$^+$) hydrogen ions** by **(OH$^-$) hydroxide ions** under **standard conditions**
$$H^+_{(aq)} + OH^-_{(aq)} \rightarrow H_2O_{(l)}$$

~ *of atomisation ΔH_{at}^Θ: is the enthalpy change when 1 mole of gaseous atoms is formed from the element in its standard state (Year 2)*
$$\tfrac{1}{2}Cl_{2(g)} \rightarrow Cl_{(g)}$$

Bond Enthalpies

or
$$\Delta H_r = \Sigma H \text{ bonds broken} - \Sigma H \text{ bonds formed}$$

$$\Delta H_r = \Sigma H \text{ bonds (reactants)} - \Sigma H \text{ bonds (products)}$$

Bond dissociation enthalpy: average bond dissociation enthalpy per mole of gaseous compound [kJ mol^{-1}]

Mean bond enthalpy: average enthalpy required to dissociate a covalent bond over different compounds.

If ΣH bonds formed $>$ ΣH bonds broken $\Rightarrow$ **exothermic**

If ΣH bonds formed $<$ ΣH bonds broken $\Rightarrow$ **endothermic**

Calorimeter

Equation; Reasons for underestimate; Diagram of calorimeter

Calorimeter

$$q = mc\Delta T$$

q: enthalpy change [Joules]
m: mass of water [g]
c: specific heat capacity of water ($4.18 \ J \ g^{-1} \ K^{-1}$ -> data sheet)
ΔT: temperature change [°C] (°C = °K)

Reasons why enthalpy change is underestimated by experiment
- Heat absorbed by container
- Heat lost to surroundings
- Incomplete combustion
- Evaporation of volatile fuel
- Non-standard conditions

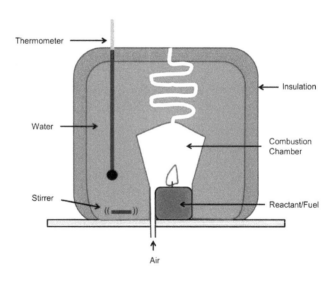

Calorimeter

Example Calculation - Neutralisation

Example Calculation - Neutralisation

30 cm^3 of 0.80 mol dm^{-3} HCl were neutralised with 20 cm^3 of 1.2 mol dm^{-3} NaOH. The temperature of the solutions increased from 20° C to 26° C. What is the enthalpy change of neutralization for this reaction?

$$HCl + NaOH \rightarrow NaCl + H_2O$$

Total volume of solution: $20 \text{ cm}^3 + 30 \text{ cm}^3 = 50 \text{ cm}^3$
Density of water: $\mathbf{1 \text{ g cm}^{-3}}$
Mass of water: $50 \text{ cm}^3 \times 1 \text{ g cm}^{-3} = 50 \text{ g}$

q = mcΔT

$q = 50 \text{ g} \times 4.18 \text{ J g}^{-1} \text{ K}^{-1} \times 6 \text{ K}$

$q = 1254 \text{ J}$

Moles water formed:

$n = 0.03 \text{ dm}^3 \times 0.8 \text{ mol dm}^{-3} = 0.024 \text{ moles}$

Enthalpy change of neutralization:

$H_{neut}^{\Theta} = 1254 \text{ J} / 0.024 \text{ moles} = -52 \text{ kJ mol}^{-1}$

**If temperature has increased -> exothermic reaction
=> put negative sign in front**

**If temperature has decreased -> endothermic reaction
=> put positive sign in front**

Hess's Law

Definition; Function; Equation; Triangles; Example Calculation

Hess's Law

The total enthalpy change for a reaction is independent of the route taken (as long as the initial and final conditions are the same)

-> To calculate enthalpy changes for unknown reactions from known reactions (e.g. reaction enthalpies from formation enthalpies)

$$\Delta H_r = \Sigma \Delta H_f \text{ (products)} - \Sigma \Delta H_f \text{ (reactants)}$$

ΔH_r : Enthalpy change of reaction [kJ mol^{-1}]
ΔH_f : Enthalpy change of formation [kJ mol^{-1}]
$\Delta H_r^{\ominus}$: Enthalpy change of reaction with elements in their standard states under standard conditions (1 atm/100 kPa, 298 K)

-> **Elements like O_2 have no formation enthalpy (zero)**

Triangles/arrows

Add arrows going to the same products (endpoint) of the unknown enthalpy ΔH_1 using the alternative route:
going along arrow -> positive sign, against arrow -> negative sign for enthalpy

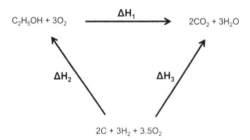

$$\Delta H_1 = -\Delta H_2 + \Delta H_3$$

Example Calculation for standard enthalpy change of combustion for ethanol:

$\Delta H_f^{\ominus} (CO_2) =$ -394 kJ mol^{-1}
$\Delta H_f^{\ominus} (H_2O) =$ -286 kJ mol^{-1}
$\Delta H_f^{\ominus} (C_2H_5OH) =$ -277 kJ mol^{-1}
$\Delta H_f^{\ominus} (C, O_2, H_2) =$ 0 kJ mol^{-1}

$\Delta H_r \quad = \Sigma \Delta H_f \text{ (products)} \quad - \quad \Sigma \Delta H_f \text{ (reactants)}$

$\Delta H_c \quad = [(2x\text{--}394) + (3x\text{-}286)] \quad - \quad [\text{-}277] \qquad | \text{ kJ mol}^{-1}$

$\qquad\quad = \textbf{-1369} \text{ kJ mol}^{-1}$

1.5 Kinetics

Rates of Reactions

Rates depend on (five bullet points); Definition & equation; Graph; Four measurement methods; Collision theory (four bullet points);Maxwell-Bolzmann distribution for temperature increase

Rates of Reactions

Rates (speed) depend on
- temperature
- surface area (size of particles)
- catalyst
- concentrations of reactants (or solvent)
- pressure for gases

Rate of reaction: change of concentration (product or reactant) over time

$$r = \frac{\Delta c}{\Delta t}$$

Graph: shows increase/decrease over time

Measurement
- Precipitation (marker disappears)
- Change in mass when gas given off (balance)
- Volume of gas given off (syringe)
- Titration

Collision Theory
- Higher temperature -> higher speed => more successful collisions (E_{kin} > E_a)
- Higher concentration -> collisions more likely
- Larger surface area -> particles can access more area
- Catalyst -> see revision card 'catalyst'

Maxwell-Bolzmann Distribution for Temperature Increase

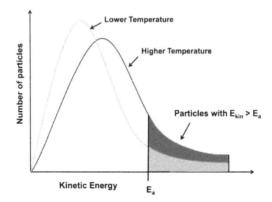

-> graphs should not touch y-axis
-> Maxwell Boltzmann distribution applies to gases only

Catalyst

Definition; (Homogeneous and heterogeneous catalysts with examples); (Catalyst poison); Steps of mechanism with diagram

Catalyst

Definition: Speeds up chemical reactions (increases rate) by **lowering activation energy** (more successful collisions) and providing an **alternative reaction pathway**.
Catalysts are **not used up** during the reactions **(unchanged).**

- *homogenous catalyst* => *same physical state as the reactants: enzymes/substrate (l/l) or H_2SO_4 (l/l) in organic chemistry (Year 2)*
- *heterogeneous catalyst* => *different physical states catalytic converter Pt/Rh (s/g) in car burns hydrocarbons and:*
  $2CO + 2NO \rightarrow 2CO_2 + N_2$
  other examples: Ni (Hydrogenation), Fe (Haber), V_2O_5 (Contact process)
  Contact process: $\quad V_2O_5 + SO_2 \rightarrow V_2O_4 + SO_3$
  $\qquad\qquad\qquad V_2O_4 + \frac{1}{2}O_2 \rightarrow V_2O_5 \rightarrow$ *Regeneration (Year 2)*
- **does not change chemical equilibrium**
- *Catalyst poison: binds stronger to catalyst than reactant -> blocking surface (Year 2)*
- **Mechanism:** $H_2 + Cl_2 \rightarrow 2HCl$
  - **adsorption** (not absorption!) of reactants (H_2, Cl_2) at catalyst surface
  - this **weakens bonds** in reactants (lowers activation energy)
  - **new bonds** of products (H-Cl) are formed
  - **desorption** of products (HCl) after reaction.

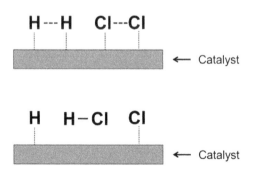

Enthalpy Profile Diagram
&
Maxwell-Boltzmann Distribution

Definition activation energy; Enthalpy profile diagram of exothermic reaction with and without catalyst; Maxwell-Boltzmann Distribution with and without catalyst

Enthalpy Profile Diagram of exothermic reaction with and without catalyst

Activation energy E_a: Minimum amount of energy needed to begin breaking reactant bonds and start a chemical reaction (positive)

Enthalpy Profile

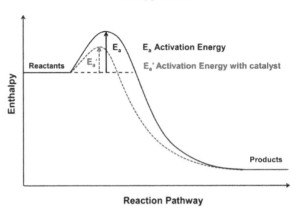

Maxwell-Boltzmann Distribution

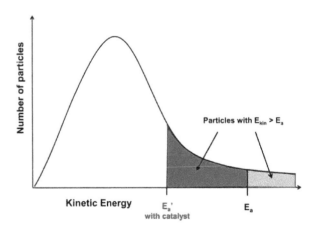

1.6 Equilibria

Equilibrium and Reversible Reactions

Definitions for reversible reaction & dynamic equilibrium; Le Chetallier; Haber process; Equilibrium law; Equilibrium constant

Equilibrium and Reversible Reactions

Reversible reaction: products convert back to reactants (reaction goes both ways) => incomplete reaction

Dynamic equilibrium (steady state)
-> rates of the forward and reverse reactions are equal
- both reactions still going on; balance => low percentage of product
- **concentrations** of reactants and products remain **constant**
- only in **closed system**

-> Important for yield in chemical industry

Le Chetallier: When the conditions of a system at equilibrium changes, the position of the equilibrium shifts in the direction that opposes (counteracts) the change

Ammonia manufacture (Haber-process): iron catalyst *(200 atm, 450 C)*

$$N_{2(g)} + 3H_{2(g)} \leftrightarrows 2NH_{3(g)} \qquad \Delta H - 93 \ kJ/mol \ (exothermic)$$

+ pressure   -> shifts to the side with less moles gas (here to the right)
+ heat   -> shifts in the direction of endothermic process (here to left)
+ concentration reactants   -> shifts to right
- concentration products   -> shifts to right

=> Catalyst does not change equilibrium but increases rate of both reactions (equilibrium is reached faster)

Equilibrium Equation

$$aA + bB \leftrightarrows cC + dD$$

Equilibrium law:

$$K_c = \frac{[C]^c [D]^d}{[A]^a [B]^b}$$

[ ]: concentration

K_c : equilibrium constant
- the larger K_c the more yield
- **K_c only temperature dependent**
- when temperature is increased then K_c increases for endothermic reactions and decreases for exothermic reactions
- need to calculate units of K_c by cancelling out units of concentration
- if concentration of [C] or [D] is increased *(numerator)*, concentration of [A] and [B] must also increase *(denominator)* to keep K_c constant (equilibrium moves to the left)
- solids (and liquids) do not appear in the equilibrium equation

Equilibrium Concentrations Calculation

Equilibrium Concentrations Calculation

-> highlight all data given **(bold)** in the question and write down mole ratios
-> create a table as specified below

0.90 moles of Nitrogen dioxide were thermally decomposed at 450 C in a container of 23 dm³. **0.40 moles** of Oxygen were found in the equilibrium mixture. Calculate K_c for this reaction.

$$2NO_2 \quad \leftrightarrows \quad 2NO \quad + \quad O_2$$

	NO_2	NO	O_2
Initial moles n_0	**0.9**		
Equilibrium moles	0.1 (n_r)	0.8 (x)	0.4 (x')
Equilibrium conc. [mol dm⁻³]	0.0043	0.035	0.017

Calculate equilibrium moles:

0.4 moles O_2 -> x'
2:1 **ratio** between NO and O_2 => 2 · 0.4 moles = 0.8 moles NO in equilibrium
1:1 (2:2) **ratio** between NO_2 and NO -> 0.8 moles NO_2 have reacted -> x
x: reacted moles of reactant (NO_2) (related to x' by mole-ratios)
Equilibrium moles of reactant (NO_2): $n_r = n_0 - x$
n_r = **0.9 mole** − 0.8 mole = 0.1 moles => 0.1 moles NO_2 left in equilibrium

Equilibrium Concentrations:

$$c = \frac{n}{V}$$

Divide all equilibrium moles by volume: e.g.

$[NO_2]$ $\frac{0.1\ mol}{23\ dm^3}$ = 0.0043 mol dm⁻³

$$K_c = \frac{[NO]^2 \times [O_2]}{[NO_2]^2} = \frac{(0.035\ )^2 \times 0.017\ mol\ dm^{-3}}{(0.0043)^2} = 1.1\ mol\ dm^{-3}$$

1.7 Redox Reactions

Redox Reactions – Oxidation States
&
Disproportionation

Definitions Oxidation/Reduction; Six rules for oxidation states; Oxidising/Reducing agent; Disproportionation

Redox reactions – Oxidation states

Oxidation Is Loss of electrons
-> oxidation state becomes more positive

Reduction Is Gain of electrons
-> oxidation state becomes more negative

=> OILRIG

Oxidation states/numbers
-> help to determine chemical formula of compound

Def: *identical to the charge of ions in a salt;*
          the charge an element would have, in a molecule, if it were a salt.

Rules:
- always zero for pure element in its basic state (uncombined element)
- group number indicates **maximum** oxidation state
- the more electronegative element gets a negative -, the less electronegative element a positive oxidation number
- the sum of all oxidation states for neutral compounds is zero

  Al_2O_3 $\quad\quad$ $(2x+3) + (3x-2) = 0$
  $_{+3\ -2}$

- the sum of all oxidation states for ions equals their charge

  SO_4^{2-} $\quad\quad$ $(+6) + (4x-2) = -2$
  $_{+6\ -2}$

- most common oxidation states in compounds:
  Halogens   -1
  Oxygen   -2 (-1)
  Hydrogen   +1 (-1)
  Metals positive (alkali metals +1, alkaline earth metals +2)

Oxidising agent: gets reduced (helps other element to get oxidised)
-> **electron acceptors**

Reducing agent: gets oxidised (helps other element to get reduced)
-> **electron donors**

Disproportionation

Definition: same element gets reduced and oxidized

-> Special kind of Redox reaction

$Cu_2O + 2H^+$ -> $Cu^{2+} + Cu + H_2O$
$_{+1}$ $\quad\quad\quad$ $_{+2}\quad _{0}$

-> see also revision card 'Water Treatment'

Balancing Redox Equations

Balancing a simple redox reaction; Balancing a complicated redox reaction; Half equations

Balancing Redox Equations

How to balance a simple redox equation
- First write the chemical formula of the product to the right side of the arrow. Balance this formula with lower case numbers according to oxidation states (group number) by using lowest common multiple.
- Then balance equation by putting numbers in front of partners (never change lower case numbers, as this would create a different substance)

$$4Al + 3O_2 \rightarrow 2Al_2O_3$$
$$0 \quad\; 0 \qquad +3\; -2 \quad \text{(lowest common multiple: 6)}$$

If not just elements reacting (ions/molecules):
- First balance electrons, starting with the biggest difference in oxidation states (between left and right side of equation)
- then balance all the other partners (oxygen before hydrogen)

$$8I^- + 8H^+ + H_2SO_4 \rightarrow 4I_2 + H_2S + 4H_2O$$
$$\;\, -1 \qquad\qquad\quad +6 \qquad\;\; 0 \quad\;\; -2$$

Biggest difference: S: $+6 \rightarrow -2$ => gains $8e^-$
I: $-1 \rightarrow 0$ => loses $1e^-$ => $8I^-$ needed

- number of electrons lost and gained must be the same!
- charges have to be balanced as well ($8I^- = 8H^+$)

Half-Equations

- split up redox reaction in two separate oxidation and reduction reactions => **half equations**
- use oxidation states to determine number of transferred electrons
- number of electrons **transferred must be the same in overall equation -> multiply to get lowest common multiple (here: 6)**

$$3Zn + 2Fe^{3+} \rightarrow 2Fe + 3Zn^{2+}$$
$$\;\;0 \qquad +3 \qquad\;\; 0 \qquad +2$$

half equations:

$$Fe^{3+} + 3e^- \rightarrow Fe \qquad\qquad | \; x\,2$$
$$Zn \rightarrow Zn^{2+} + 2e^- \qquad\quad | \; x\,3$$

Two Main Types of Inorganic Reactions
&
Ionic Equations

*Two main types and two minor types of inorganic reactions;
Definition of spectator ion*

Two Main Types of Inorganic Reactions

1) Redox (Reduction/Oxidation)
-> transfer of electrons (Oxidation states change)

$$4Al + 3O_2 -> 2Al_2O_3$$
$$0 \quad\quad 0 \quad\quad\quad +3\ -2$$

-> **Displacement** & **Disproportionation** are special cases of Redox reactions

2) Acid-Base
-> transfer of protons H^+ (Oxidation states do not change)

$$HCl + NaOH -> NaCl + H_2O$$
$$+1\ -1 \quad +1\ -2\ +1 \quad\ +1\ -1 \quad\ +1\ -2$$

Minor reaction types

- Thermal decomposition
  $$CaCO_{3(s)} -> CaO_{(s)} + CO_{2(g)}$$

- Precipitation
  $$Ag^+_{(aq)} + Cl^-_{(aq)} -> AgCl_{(s)}$$

-> No change of oxidation states

Ionic equations

Spectator Ions: Ions which do not take part in the reaction
They can be removed from the full equation to give an ionic equation

Full equation:
$$Cl_2 + 2NaBr -> Br_2 + 2NaCl$$
$$0 \quad +1\ -1 \quad\quad 0 \quad\ +1\ -1$$

Na^+ does not change oxidation states -> spectator ion, can be removed from equation =>

Ionic equation:
$$Cl_2 + 2Br^- -> Br_2 + 2Cl^-$$
$$0 \quad\ -1 \quad\quad 0 \quad\quad -1$$

Unit 2 – Inorganic Chemistry

2.1 Periodicity

Periodic Table
&
Periodic Trends

*Group and Period number; Group names; Blocks; Mendeleev;
Elements existing as diatomic molecules;
Trends across the period: atomic radius, electronegativity,
ionisation energy, melting & boiling points*

Periodic Table

-> arranged by proton number

Group number
-> number of outer electrons => determines chemical properties & reactions

Period number
-> number of shells

Group Names

Gr 1	**Alkali metals**
Gr 2	**Alkaline earth metals**
Gr 7	**Halogens**
Gr 8	**Noble Gases**
Gr III – XII	**Transition metals**

s-block: Group 1,2
p-block: Group 3 - 8
d-block: Transition elements
-> named after the outer subshell

Mendeleev
- Early version of periodic table: Elements arranged by atomic mass
- Left gaps to have elements with similar chemical properties in same group

Elements existing as diatomic molecules
H_2, N_2, O_2, Halogens: F_2, Cl_2, Br_2, I_2 *(Have No Fear Of Ice-Cold Beer)*

Periodic Trends

Atomic radius decreases across period
- More protons (nuclear charge) -> electrons pulled closer
- Same shell -> no extra shielding

Electronegativity & Ionisation energy increase across period
-> see flashcards 'Electronegativity' & Ionisation Enthalpy'

Melting and Boiling points
- Increase for metals across period -> see revision card "Metallic Bond'
- Still increase for group 4 elements -> rev. card 'Giant Covalent Structures'
- Then increase or decrease for non-metals depending on how many atoms form simple covalent structure (van der Waals forces) -> see revision cards 'Simple Covalent Structures' & 'Elements existing as diatomic molecules'
- Noble gases have lowest melting points due to existing as single atoms

Ionisation Energy

Definition of Ionisation Enthalpy; Trends across period and down group (three bullet points);Reactivities;1st and 2nd ionisation enthalpies; Drops in ionisation enthalpies

Ionisation Energy

Definition: Energy required to remove one electron from **one mole** of atoms of an element in the **gaseous state** [kJ/mol]

Increases across period:
- more protons
- same shell
- smaller radius
  => stronger nuclear attraction

Decreases down group:
- more shells, more distance
- more shielding
- despite more protons

Reactivity
- decreases down Halogen group
- increases down Alkali group

1st Ionisation energy: $\qquad O_{(g)} \rightarrow O^+_{(g)} + e^-$

2nd Ionisation energy: $\qquad O^+_{(g)} \rightarrow O^{2+}_{(g)} + e^-$

2nd Ionisation energy > 1st Ionisation energy
- increasingly positive ion
- smaller ions
- less repulsion amongst remaining electrons

Big jump when new shell is broken into => closer to the nucleus

Drop in ionisation energy between Groups 2 (Be) and 3 (B)
-> start of p-subshell, which is further away from nucleus
-> full $2s^2$ subshell gives some partial shielding
-> despite increased nuclear charge

Drop between Groups 5 (N) and 6 (O)
-> one orbital of the three p-orbitals is filled with two, paired electrons, which repel each other

2.2 Group 2 The Alkaline Earth Metals

Group 2 Alkaline Earth Metals

Reactions with water, oxygen and acids; Oxides & hydroxides; Reduction of titanium oxide; Solubility trends; Test for sulphates; Barium meals; Periodic trends

Group 2 Alkaline Earth Metals

Reactions of the Alkaline Earth Metals

React with water to produce hydroxides and hydrogen gas
$$Mg_{(s)} + 2H_2O_{(l)} \to Mg(OH)_{2(aq)} + H_{2(g)}$$

They burn in oxygen with characteristic colour
$$2Ca_{(s)} + O_{2(g)} \to 2CaO_{(s)} \quad \text{(brick red)}$$
Mg -> brilliant white flame

Group 2 oxides & hydroxides are bases
- $Mg(OH)_2$ neutralises stomach acid (indigestion tablets)
- $Ca(OH)_2$ neutralises acid soils (agriculture)
-> see revision card 'bases'

Magnesium is used for the reduction of titanium oxide (TiO_2)
1) $TiO_{2(s)} + 2Cl_{2(g)} + 2C_{(s)} \to TiCl_{4(s)} + 2CO_{(g)}$ (900 C)
2) Fractional distillation of $TiCl_{4(s)}$ under Ar or N_2
3) $TiCl_{4(s)} + 2Mg_{(l)} \to Ti_{(s)} + 2MgCl_{2(l)}$ (furnace, 1000 C)

Solubility trends of Group 2 metals
Singly charged anions (OH^-)   -> increased solubility down group
double charged anions (SO_4^{2-}) -> decreased solubility down group

Hydroxides	more soluble down group
Sulphates	less soluble
Carbonates	less soluble

Test for sulphate or Ba^{2+} ions: add acidified (removes carbonate) $BaCl_2$ solution
$$Ba^{2+}_{(aq)} + SO_4^{2-}_{(aq)} \to BaSO_{4(s)} \qquad \textbf{white precipitate}$$

Barium meals
- Barium sulphate absorbs X-rays.
- Used in medicine to show soft tissue in X-rays.
- Nontoxic: does not enter blood stream due to insolubility.

Periodic Trends of Alkaline Earth Metals

Atomic & Ionic Radius increases down group
-> more shells

Ionisation Energy decreases down group
=> Reactivity increases down group
-> see revision card 'Ionisation energy'

Melting Points decrease down group
-> see revision card 'Metallic bonding'

2.3 Group 7 The Halogens

Group 7 Halogens
&
Water Treatment

Halogens characteristics and trends;
Water treatment with chlorine; Bleach; (Iodine tables), Fluoride

Group 7 Halogens

-> Diatomic molecules

F_2	yellow gas	very toxic	
Cl_2	green gas	toxic	bleaches litmus paper
Br_2	red-brown liquid	toxic	
I_2	black-purple solid		

Strong oxidizing agents
Metal + Halogen -> Halide salts (redox)
$2Na + Cl_2 -> 2NaCl$

Less electronegative down group
-> see revision card 'Electronegativity'

Less reactive down group
-> see revision card 'Ionization energy'

Melting/boiling point increase down group
- larger molecules
- more electrons
-> stronger London forces

Water treatment

Water treatment (drinking water/swimming pool)
$Cl_2 + H_2O -> HClO + HCl ->$ Disproportionation -> see revision card
   0   +1   -1

HClO chloric(I) acid *(hypochlorous acid)* -> dissociates into H^+ and ClO^- ions
ClO^- chlorate(I) ion is strong oxidising agent which kills bacteria and algae

Disadvantages:
- Cl_2 harmful and toxic –> irritates respiratory system; liquid chlorine burns skin/eyes
- Cl_2 reacts with organic compounds to form chlorinated hydrocarbons –> carcinogenic

Bleach Preparation
$Cl_2 + 2NaOH -> NaClO + NaCl + H_2O$
Condition: cold, dilute sodiumhydroxide

Bleach: NaClO Sodium chlorate(I) - strong oxidising agent (disinfectant)

Iodine tablets (camping – drinking water)
$I_2 + H_2O -> HI + HIO$

F^- ions prevent tooth decay

Halides

Silver nitrate test; Reducing agent; Reactions with sulphuric acid: NaF/NaCl, NaBr, NaI; Hydrogen halides

Halides

Test for Halide Ions

-> with acidified (HNO_3 -> removes carbonates) **$AgNO_3$** solution:

Halide	Precipitate	Dissolves in	
F^-	-		
Cl^-	white	diluted NH_3	*(complex)*
Br^-	cream	conc NH_3	*(complex)*
I^-	yellow	insoluble	

Displacement reactions
-> other test for halides -> See revision card 'Displacement'

Reducing agent
-> power increases down group (more shells, more shielding)

Reactions of Halide ions with H_2SO_4

NaF or NaCl with H_2SO_4:
$NaF_{(s)}$ + $H_2SO_{4(aq)}$ -> $NaHSO_{4(s)}$ + $HF_{(g)}$ -> acid/base reaction
$NaCl_{(s)}$ + $H_2SO_{4(aq)}$ -> $NaHSO_{4(s)}$ + $HCl_{(g)}$ **-> test for HCl see below**

NaBr with H_2SO_4
$NaBr_{(s)}$ + $H_2SO_{4(aq)}$ -> $NaHSO_{4(s)}$ + $HBr_{(g)}$
$2HBr_{(aq)}$ + $H_2SO_{4(aq)}$ -> $SO_{2(g)}$ + $2H_2O_{(l)}$ + $Br_{2(g)}$ -> Brown **Fumes** (redox)
   $_{-1}$ $_{+6}$ $_{+4}$ $_{0}$

NaI with H_2SO_4
$NaI_{(s)}$ + $H_2SO_{4(aq)}$ -> $NaHSO_{4(s)}$ + $HI_{(g)}$
$2HI_{(g)}$ + $H_2SO_{4(aq)}$ -> $SO_{2(g)}$ + $2H_2O_{(l)}$ + $I_{2(g)}$ -> Purple **vapour** (redox)
  $_{-1}$ $_{+6}$ $_{+4}$ $_{0}$

$6HI_{(g)}$ + $SO_{2(g)}$ -> $H_2S_{(g)}$ + $3I_{2(s)}$ + $2H_2O_{(l)}$ -> H_2S: **toxic, smelly gas**
  $_{-1}$ $_{+4}$ $_{-2}$ $_{0}$

Hydrogen Halides

- Colourless acidic gases
- turn blue litmus paper red
- Test for HCl:
  $NH_{3(g)}$ + $HCl_{(g)}$ -> $NH_4Cl_{(s)}$ -> white fumes

Test for Ions
&
Displacement Reaction
&
Solubility

Tests for carbonates, sulphates, ammonium & halides;
Displacement reaction with equation and table;
Common insoluble & soluble salts; Solvents

Test for Ions

Carbonates: $CO_3^{2-} + 2H^+ \rightarrow H_2O + CO_2$ fizzing, **carbonate disappears**

Sulphates: $Ba^{2+}_{(aq)} + SO_4^{2-}_{(aq)} \rightarrow BaSO_{4(s)}$ **white precipitate**

Ammonium: $NH_4^+ + OH^- \rightarrow H_2O + NH_3$ **litmus: red -> blue**

Halides: $Ag^+_{(aq)} + X^-_{(aq)} \rightarrow AgX_{(s)}$ **precipitate**

X^-: halide ion (Cl⁻, Br⁻, I⁻)   -> see revision card 'Halides'

Displacement Reaction

- to identify halide ions
- more reactive halogen displaces (oxidises) less reactive
  -> higher up in group => higher oxidizing strength
- special type of redox reaction
- shake solution with hexane or cyclohexane (non-polar solvents, better for dissolving halogen)

$$Cl_2 + 2Br^- \rightarrow Br_2 + 2Cl^-$$
$$\scriptstyle 0 \qquad -1 \qquad\quad 0 \qquad -1$$

	Water	Hexane
F_2 yellow gas	-	-
Cl_2 green gas	colourless	pale green
Br_2 red-brown liquid	yellow/orange	orange/red
I_2 black-purple solid	brown	pink/violet

Solubility

How soluble a salt is depends on its characteristics *(K_{sp}-solubility product constant)* and cannot usually be predicted from its chemical formula, but can be experimentally determined.

Common insoluble salts:
- silver halides
- barium sulphate
- most carbonates - except sodium, potassium, ammonium carbonates

Common soluble salts:
- most hydrogen carbonates like $NaHCO_3$ (baking soda)
- most sodium salts

Solvents:
- salts and polar molecules are soluble in polar solvents like water
- non polar molecules like halogens or hydrocarbons are soluble in non-polar solvents like cyclohexane

List of Anions
&
Naming Salts

Eleven anions;
Rule for naming cations; Four rules for naming anions

List of Anions

chloride	Cl^-
carbonate	CO_3^{2-}
hydroxide	OH^-
sulphate	SO_4^{2-}
sulphate(IV)/sulphite	SO_3^{2-}
sulphide	S^{2-}
nitrate	NO_3^-
nitrate(IV)/nitrite	NO_2^-
phosphate	PO_4^{3-}
ethanoate/acetate	CH_3COO^-
cyanide	CN^-

Naming salts

First cation (metal, +) then anion (non-metal, -): e.g. NaCl -> sodium chloride

Oxidation number of the cation (positive ion) is written in **roman numerals** in brackets in the salt name to distinguish different salts, e.g. Iron(**II**) sulphate: $FeSO_4$, Iron(**III**) sulphate: $Fe_2(SO_4)_3$

Name of **anion (negative ion)** finishes with:

- **ide** -> if anion consists of just one element like S^{2-}, e.g. Ca**S** – calcium sulph**ide** or NaCl – sodium chlor**ide**

- **ate** -> anion consists of more than one elements like SO_4^{2-} (sulphur & oxygen) and sulphur is in its highest oxidation state (+6): e. g. Na$_2$**SO$_4$** – Sodium sulph**ate** -> or **sulphate(VI)**

- **ite** -> anion with more than one element (sulphur & oxygen) and sulphur is in its second highest oxidation state (+4) for example Na_2SO_3 – Sodium sulf**ite** -> or **sulphate(IV)**
-> **SO_3^{2-} can also be named sulphate(IV): write oxidation state as roman numeral in brackets**
=> use this as general method for naming anions with more than one element

2.4 – Investigative and Practical Skills

Accuracy and Reliability
&
Percentage of Uncertainty

Definitions

Accuracy and Reliability

Accuracy: How close the result is to the true value

Reliability: How reproducible the result is

- The more times an experiment is repeated the more reliable the results become.
- This reduces the effect of random errors (e.g. limitation of accuracy of pipette: getting 49.9 ml or 50.1 ml when measuring 50 ml)
- But the result can still be wrong due to a systematic error (e.g. wrong calibration of a balance -> always 0.5 g to heavy).

Percentage of Uncertainty

Definition: The uncertainty in a single measurement from a single instrument is **half the least count (unit) of the instrument**

-> add uncertainties of each instrument together

Example:
- burette with 0.1 ml graduation => +/- 0.05 ml (maximum error)
  -> 0.05 ml uncertainty
- two readings (before and after titration) two times uncertainty
  2×0.05 ml = 0.1 ml total uncertainty for the titration
- if 10 ml of standard solution was used for the titration then uncertainty:
  0.1 ml/10 ml = 1.0 % of this volume reading

Acids
&
Bases

Definition for acid; Important acids; Reaction with metals;
Difference between weak and strong acids;
Definition for base, Four types of bases; Definition alkali; Tests
for acids & bases; (Rules for anions)

Acids

Definition (Bronsted-Lowry): Acid –> proton (H^+) donor

Important acids:

HCl	hydrochloric acid (hydrogen chloride) - s
H_2SO_4	sulphuric acid - s
HNO_3	nitric acid - s
H_2CO_3	carbonic acid - w
CH_3COOH	ethanoic acid, acetic acid - w
H_3PO_4	phosphoric acid - w

Acids reacting with metals forming hydrogen (Redox)
$$Mg + H_2SO_4 \rightarrow MgSO_4 + H_2$$

Strong acids (s): Completely dissociated:
$$HCl \rightarrow H^+ + Cl^-$$

Weak acids (w): Partially dissociated:
$$CH_3COOH \rightleftarrows CH_3COO^- + H^+$$
=> equilibrium (less H^+ ions)

Bases

-> Proton (H^+) acceptor

Metal oxides
$MgO + 2HCl \rightarrow MgCl_2 + H_2$ **Indigestion tablets**

Hydroxides
$Ca(OH)_2 + 2HCl \rightarrow CaCl_2 + 2H_2O$ **Neutralises acid soils;**
                                                Removes HCl-fumes

Ammonia
$NH_3 + HCl \rightarrow NH_4Cl$ Fertilizer

Carbonates
$CaCO_3 + 2HCl \rightarrow CaCl_2 + H_2O + CO_2$ Fizzing, $CaCO_3$ **disappears**
=> **acid test**

An **Alkali** is a soluble base (base that dissolves in water and releases OH^-)

Tests for acids and bases:
- pH indicator changes colour (litmus red -> blue base; blue -> red acid)
- pH meter shows value lower (acid) or greater (base) than 7

-> Anion of weak acid is a base (-> conjugated base)
*-> Anion of strong acid is **not** a base*

Acids and Bases Preparation
&
Preparing a Standard Solution

Preparing acids; Preparing bases
Steps for preparing a standard solution

Acids and Bases preparation

Acids:
Non-metal-oxide   + H₂O   ->   Acid
CO_2 $+ H_2O$ -> H_2CO_3
-> Non-metal-oxides are hidden acids (Lewis acid)

Base:
Metaloxide   + H₂O   ->   Metalhydroxide
CaO $+ H_2O$ -> $Ca(OH)_2$
-> Metal oxides are hidden hydroxides/bases (Lewis base)

Preparing a Standard Solution

- calculate moles of compound from volume and concentration by using $n = c \ V$

- calculate mass of compound by using $m = n \ M$

- place a plastic weighing boat (dish) or weighing paper on a digital balance and zero the balance (tare)

- weigh the compound to an appropriate number of decimal places (e. g. 0.01)

- if the solid compound has been stored in the fridge allow it to reach room temperature before opening the bottle

- transfer the compound into a beaker which already contains some solvent (distilled H_2O) -> around 80 % of the final volume (e. g. 80 ml of 100 ml final volume)

- the solvent should be at room temperature

- rinse the weighing boat with distilled water to transfer the remaining compound, sticking to the boat, into the beaker

- dissolve by stirring the mixture, of compound and solvent, in the beaker

- if it's necessary to heat or cool to aid dissolving, ensure the solution has reached room temperature before the next step

- transfer the solution to a volumetric flask using a funnel

- rinse the beaker and stirrer and add the washing water into the flask

- slowly add distilled water up to the calibration mark of the flask (bottom of the meniscus)

- insert stopper and shake thoroughly to ensure complete mixing

- label the flask

Titrations

Purpose; Indicators; Endpoint; Steps; Accuracy of volume measurement

Titrations

-> method to determine a concentration

Acid-Base Titration (Neutralization)

Indicator *(weak organic acid)*
- indicates pH jump by colour change at endpoint
- pH range over which indicator changes colour is approximately two pH units *(pK_a(In) +/- 1)*

phenolphthalein:	**colourless (a)**	-> pink **(b)**
methyl orange:	**red (a)**	-> yellow **(b)**
not universal indicator	-> too gradual colour change	

Endpoint, equivalence point (same number of moles of H^+ & OH^-)
-> pH of indicator colour change *(pka)* must match equivalence point:
- Weak base with strong acid   -> methyl orange *(pka = 3.5)*
- Weak acid with strong base   -> phenolphthalein *(pka = 9.3)*
- Strong acid with strong base   -> any indicator

Titration Steps

- clean burette by flushing with distilled H_2O and standard solution (water dilutes standard)
- fill burette with standard solution above 0 and drain to 0 mark (removes air bubbles in tap)
- fill exact volume of unknown solution, with volumetric pipette, in conical flask
- add few drops of indicator (too much indicator would change pH)
- use white tile as background
- do rough titration to get an idea for the endpoint
- do accurate titration and repeat at least three times (reliability)
- record volumes of standard solution used (eyes level, bottom of meniscus)
- calculate the average volume
- calculate moles of standard solution from volume using $n = c\,V$
- calculate concentration of unknown solution by using $c = n/V$

Accuracy of volume measurement
volumetric pipette > graduated pipette > burette > measuring cylinder

Unit 3 - Organic Chemistry

3.1 Introduction to Organic Chemistry

Naming Rules
&
Types of Organic Formulae

Eight naming rules with example; Types of formulae: molecular, structural, displayed, skeletal, general

Naming Rules (Nomenclature)

- Longest chain –> forms the middle or beginning of the name (pentan-2-ol)
- Choose longest chain with **most side-chains**
- **Numbering carbons**: lowest number for functional groups/side chains
- Never put side-chain (branched chain) on first or last carbon (creates not an isomer, just makes the chain longer)
- **Side-chains** (alkyl groups): Methyl, Ethyl, Propyl, Butyl,...
  –> put at beginning of name with carbon number and dash in front (**3-ethyl-2,4-dimethyl**pentane)
- Alphabetical order for alkyl side chains (disregard di, tri, ...)
  (3-ethyl-2,4-dimethylpentane)
- Multiple side-chains/functional groups: di, tri, tetra, ...*(2, 3, 4,...)*
- Main functional group –> ending of name (pentan-2-ol)

Example:

3-ethyl-2,4-dimethylpentan-2-ol

Types of Organic Formulae

2-methylpentan-1-ol:

molecular formula: $C_6H_{14}O$

structural formula: $CH_3CH_2CH_2CH(CH_3)CH_2OH$

displayed formula/structural formula (all bonds must be drawn):

skeletal formula:

General formula for all alcohols: $C_nH_{2n+1}OH$

Functional Groups

Definition; Alcohol; Aldehyde; Ketone; Carboxylic acid; Ester; (Ether); Amine; (Amide); (Nitro)

Functional Groups

Definition: Group of atoms in a molecule that is responsible for the reaction

R (residue): alkyl-group C_nH_{2n+1} : $-CH_3$ (methyl), $-C_2H_5$ (ethyl), $-C_3H_7$ (propyl) etc.

Alcohol   R-OH

Aldehyde

$$R-C\underset{H}{\overset{O}{\nearrow}}$$

Ketone

$$R^1-C\underset{R^2}{\overset{O}{\nearrow}}$$

Carboxylic Acid

$$R-C\underset{OH}{\overset{O}{\nearrow}}$$

Ester

$$R^1-C\underset{O-R^2}{\overset{O}{\nearrow}}$$

Ether R^1-O-R^2

Amine $R-NH_2$

Amide (Peptide)

$$R^1-C\underset{NH-R^2}{\overset{O}{\nearrow}}$$

Nitro $R-NO_2$

Nitrile   R-CN

Three Main Types of Organic Reactions and Mechanisms

Three main types of organic reactions with examples; Three main reaction mechanisms with word explanations; Electrophiles & nucleophiles: definitions and examples; Hydrolysis & condensation

Three Main Types of Organic Reactions

Substitution   (e.g. haloalkane with OH^-)
Elimination   (e.g. dehydration of alcohol)
Addition   (e.g. HX on double bond of alkenes)

(Oxidation/Reduction -> inorganic)
(acid base reaction / salt formation -> inorganic)

Three Main Organic Reaction Mechanisms

nucleophilic   (likes positive charges)
electrophilic   (likes electrons/negative charges)
radical   (unpaired electron, very aggressive)

Electrophiles & Nucleophiles

Electrophiles
-> **electron pair acceptors**
- Cations: H^+, X^+, NO_2^+
- or induced dipole molecules like halogens X_2 (Br_2)

Nucleophiles
-> **electron pair donors**
-> **possess at least one lone pair of electrons (ideally anions)**
- OH^-, CN^-, X^-, NH_3, H_2O, R-OH

Hydrolysis & Condensation

Hydrolysis:
breaking of covalent bonds by reaction with water (or adding H^+/OH^-)

Condensation:
reaction in which two molecules combine to form a larger one and in which water or another small molecule (HCl, methanol, acetic acid) is formed (lost).

Types of Isomers

Two main types of isomers with definitions; Three and two subtypes with examples; Conditions for E/Z isomerism; Shape; Priority rule

Types of Isomers

I) Structural Isomers

Definition: same molecular formula but different structural formula

    1) Chain-Isomers –> chain arranged differently

$$CH_3$$
$$|$$
H$_3$C—CH$_2$—CH$_2$—CH$_3$ H$_3$C—CH—CH$_3$

        butane   2-methylpropane

    2) Positional Isomers –> functional group at different positions

        OH   OH
        | |
H$_3$C—CH$_2$—CH$_2$ H$_3$C—HC—CH$_3$

      propan-1-ol   propan-2-ol

    3) Functional Group Isomers –> different functional groups

H$_3$C—CH$_2$—C(=O)H   H$_3$C—C(=O)—CH$_3$

      propanal   propanone
    other examples: alcohol/ether, carboxylic acid/ester

II) Stereoisomers

Definition: same structural formula but atoms arranged differently in space

    1) E/Z isomerism (Cis/Trans – if just two different groups)
      Cond.: Double bond (can't rotate) & at least **2 different atoms/groups**
        attached to two different carbon atoms

    Shape: trigonal planar, 120°

    H   CH$_3$ H   H
      C=C   C=C
  H$_3$C   H   H$_3$C   CH$_3$

      E (trans)   **Z (cis)**

    Cahn-Ingold-Prelog: the higher **atomic number** the higher **priority**

          2.
    F   Br   F   Cl
      C=C   C=C
   I   Cl   I   Br
  1.   1.   2.
    E (trans)   **Z (cis)**

    2) Optical Isomers -> see Year 2 revision card

3.2 Alkanes

Alkanes
&
Terms

Definition; Homologues series; Characteristics and reactions; Application; Preparation;
Terms: Homologues series, aliphatic, aromatic, alicyclic

Alkanes

Saturated **hydrocarbons** (only single C-C bonds, **only hydrogen and carbon**)

Homologues series of alkanes: $C_n H_{2n+2}$
Methane, Ethane, Propane, Butane   -> gases
Pentane, Hexane, Heptane, Octane, Nonane, Decane   -> liquids
from C_{18}   *-> solid*

- unreactive
- only other organic reactions: **radical substitution**/*elimination*
- branched isomers have lower boiling point than unbranched
  - less surface area of contact
  - weaker Van der Waals forces
  - less energy required to overcome Van der Waals forces

Application
Fuel: Burning/combustion with O_2 -> CO_2 + H_2O
               -> side product NO_x (toxic)
Limited supply of O_2 => incomplete combustion:
                            => unburned hydrocarbons & CO (toxic)
Fuel contains sulphur => SO_2 (pollution, acid rain), removed with CaO or
$CaCO_3$ in gas scrubbers: SO_2 + CaO -> $CaSO_3$ *(neutralization)*

Preparation
from crude oil

Terms

Homologues series: Group of compound with same general formula and same functional group. They differ by a 'CH_2' group

Aliphatic: A compound containing carbon and hydrogen joined together in straight chains, branched chains or non-aromatic rings

Alicyclic: An aliphatic compound arranged in non-aromatic rings with or without side chains

Crude Oil – Fuel
&
Greenhouse Effect

Separation of crude oil fractions; List of fractions; Cracking including thermal and catalytic cracking
Greenhouse effect: greenhouse gases with three bullet points

Crude Oil – Fuel

- crude oil consists of hydrocarbons with different chain length.
- in a petroleum refinery, these are separated, in different fractions, according to their boiling point by fractional distillation (heating then cooling in tower -> condensation)
- the longer the chain the higher the boiling point (bottom of fractionating/ cooling tower)

different fractions:

<RT	Gases	$C_1 - C_4$	LPG, camping gas
< 40 C	Petrol (gasoline)	$C_5 - C_{12}$	petrol
<110 C	Naphtha	$C_7 - C_{14}$	petrochemicals
<180 C	Kerosene (paraffin)	$C_{11} - C_{15}$	jet fuel
<250 C	Gas-Oil (diesel)	$C_{15} - C_{19}$	diesel, central heating
<340 C	Mineral-Oil	$C_{20} - C_{30}$	lubricating oil
>350 C	Residue: Fuel-Oil	$C_{30} - C_{40}$	ships, power stations
	Wax, Grease	$C_{40} - C_{50}$	candles, lubrication
	Bitumen	C_{50+}	road, roofing

Cracking
long chains are broken down by Cracking to produce more small and middle chains,
-> More demand for petrol ($C_4 - C_{10}$), naphtha ($C_7 - C_{14}$ – petrochemicals) & alkenes

Thermal Cracking
thermal decomposition through heating (high temperature & high pressure)
Naphtha -> alkenes (for plastics) & side products (alkanes – straight/ branched/ cyclic)

Catalytic Cracking
Thermal decomposition (450° C) with steam and catalyst Al_2O_3 (zeolite) under slight pressure
Bitumen -> fuel & arenes

Greenhouse effect

Greenhouse gases:
- H_2O, CO_2, CH_4
- absorb IR radiation -> bonds vibrate
- cause global warming

3.3 Haloalkanes

Radical Substitution in Alkanes

Definition for radical; Types of fission; Three steps of radical substitution; Curly arrows; Overall reaction

Radical Substitution in Alkanes

Radical: species with unpaired electron

Homolytic fission: each atom receives one bond electron, radicals are formed

$$Cl - Cl \xrightarrow{UV} Cl \cdot + Cl \cdot$$

Heterolytic fission: one atom receives both bond electrons, ions are formed

$$Cl - Cl \rightarrow Cl^- + Cl^+$$

Initiation:

$$Cl - Cl \xrightarrow{UV} Cl \cdot + Cl \cdot$$

A few radicals are formed by photodisssociation (most of Cl_2 still intact)

Propagation (chain reaction)

$$H-\overset{\overset{\displaystyle H}{|}}{\underset{\underset{\displaystyle H}{|}}{C}}-H \ + \ Cl \cdot \longrightarrow CH_3 \cdot \ + \ HCl$$

$$CH_3 \cdot \ + \ Cl-Cl \longrightarrow H_3C-Cl \ + \ Cl \cdot$$

- radical substitution of H atoms with halogen atoms => haloalkanes
- chain reaction continues until all H are substituted
=> **mixture of products**: monochloro-, dichloro-, trichloromethane and tetrachloromethane

Curly arrows:
- **full headed - movement of a pair of electrons**
- **half headed - movement of a single electron**

Termination:

$$Cl \cdot \ + \ Cl \cdot \longrightarrow Cl-Cl$$

$$CH_3 \cdot \ + \ CH_3 \cdot \longrightarrow H_3C-CH_3$$

$$CH_3 \cdot \ + \ Cl \cdot \longrightarrow H_3C-Cl$$

Overall reaction:

$$CH_4 \ + \ Cl_2 \ \rightarrow \ CH_3Cl \ + \ HCl$$

Ozone Layer and CFCs

Definition radical; (Two equations for ozone formation);
Equations for breakdown of ozone layer by CFCs and NO_x;
Alternatives to CFCs

Ozone Layer and CFCs

Radical: unpaired (single) electron (highly reactive)
=> see also revision card 'Radical Substitution on Alkanes'

Ozone in upper atmosphere *(stratosphere)* protects us
-> absorbs UV radiation which damages body

Ozone layer is constantly replaced:

$O_2 + hv\ (UV) \rightarrow O^{\cdot} + O^{\cdot}$

$O_2 + O^{\cdot} \leftrightarrows O_3$

CFCs (chlorofluorocarbons) and NO_x break down ozone layer:

Initiation:

$CFCl_3 \rightarrow CFCl_2^{\cdot} + Cl^{\cdot}$ (UV)

Propagation:

$R^{\cdot} + O_3 \rightarrow RO^{\cdot} + O_2$

$RO^{\cdot} + O_3 \rightarrow R^{\cdot} + 2O_2$

-> Radical **R**$^{\cdot}$ is regenerated (R = X$^{\cdot}$ or NO$^{\cdot}$) => catalyst

- CFCs used as **solvents** and propellants
  They are inert and very stable -> live long enough to reach stratosphere
- Montreal protocol to reduce CFCs and protect ozone layer
- **Alternatives**: HCFC (hydrochlorofluorocarbons) **& HFC & Hydrocarbons**
  less stable -> broken down before reaching ozone layer

Haloalkanes

Preparation; Naming; Reactivity; Characteristics of R-X group; Four hydrolysis reactions with mechanism; Elimination

Haloalkanes (Halogenoalkanes)

Can be made by radical substitution of alkanes -> see revision card 'Radical Substitution on Alkanes'

Naming

$$\begin{array}{ccc} Cl & Br \\ | & | \\ H-C-C-H \\ | & | \\ H & H \end{array}$$

2-Bromo-1-Chloroethane (alphabetically)

Reactivity

- $I > Br > Cl > F$
- bigger halogen atom -> weaker C-X bond, more reactive, higher rate
- tested with hot $AgNO_3$ -> precipitations at different rates

C-X polar bond (different electronegativities) => **X good leaving group** -> likes to undergo **nucleophilic substitution**

Mechanism:

-> heterolytic fission of haloalkane (hydrolysis)

Hydrolysis of Haloalkanes: nucleophilic substitution

$R\text{-}X + OH^- \rightarrow R\text{-}OH + X^-$
Conditions: Warm aqueous diluted sodium hydroxide solution

$R\text{-}X + H_2O \rightarrow R\text{-}OH + HX$
Conditions: Warming

$R\text{-}X + 2NH_3 \rightarrow R\text{-}NH_2 + NH_4X$
Conditions: Heating, reflux, pressure, in ethanol

$R\text{-}X + KCN \rightarrow R\text{-}CN + KX$
Cond.: Warm, KCN in ethanol => nitrile => *increase of chain length*

Elimination -> competing with substitution
-> favoured when more heating, reflux, anhydrous (ethanol) and conc. NaOH
-> OH^- acts as **base** for H^+ from hydrocarbon

3.4 Alkenes

Alkenes – Reaction with Halogens

Definition; General formula; Naming; Characteristics & reactions of double bond; Mechanism for halogenation reaction; Test for alkenes

Alkenes – Reaction with Halogens

Unsaturated hydrocarbons (C=C double bonds) -> reactive

General Formula: C_nH_{2n} -> same as cyclic Alkanes

Naming:

$$H_3C\underset{1}{}-\underset{2}{CH}=\underset{3}{CH}-\underset{4}{CH_3}$$

but-2-ene

double bond: **high electron density** => **electrophilic Addition**

Reactions:

Halogenation – electrophilic Addition

Addition of Halogens (X_2: F_2, Cl_2, Br_2, I_2)

Alkene + X_2 -> Halogenoalkane (disubstituted)

-> bromine (brown-red) gets decolourised
Conditions: spontaneous at RT (room temperature)

Mechanism:

Induced dipole   Carbocation   1,2 dibromoethane
-> heterolytic fission

Test for alkenes:
Shake with bromine water at RT: orange -> colourless

Alkenes - Addition of Hydrogen Halides

Mechanism for hydrogen halide addition; Markovnikov's rule

Alkenes - Addition of Hydrogen Halides

Alkene + HX -> Halogenoalkane (monosubstituted)

Mechanism:

permanent dipole   secondary carbocation   2-bromopropane
(major)

1-bromopropane (minor product)

Markovnikov's **rule for electrophilic Addition on unsymmetrical alkene with H-X (e.g. H-Br):**
Halide (X^-) will go to carbon with more alkyl groups, H^+ will go to carbon with less alkyl substituents

Reason: Alkyl groups (primary < secondary < tertiary) stabilize carbocation by pushing electrons down *(Inductive (+I) effect)*

Alkenes – Hydration and Fermentation

Hydration reaction; Steam hydration; Mechanism of hydration with sulphuric acid, Table hydration/fermentation; Three conditions for fermentation; Fermentation reaction; Applications; Carbon neutral

Alkenes – Hydration and Fermentation

Hydration to produce alcohols

$$\text{Ethene} \quad + \quad H_2O \quad \rightleftharpoons \quad \text{Ethanol} \quad \text{(electrophilic addition)}$$

1) Steam Hydration
Condition: acid catalyst H_3PO_4 (on silica), $300\degree$ C (exothermic), $60 - 70$ atm
Equilibrium with low yield -> unreacted ethene is separated and recycled back into reactor

2) Hydration with sulfuric acid (catalyst) and warm water

Compare with fermentation

Method	Rate	Quality	Material	Process
Hydration	Very fast	Pure	Ethene (crude oil)	Continuous, expensive equipment, low labour
Fermentation	Very slow	Impure	Sugars (renewable)	Batch, cheap, high labour

Conditions for fermentation:
- yeast
- anaerobic
- correct Temperature: $30 - 40\degree$ C

Fermentation reaction: $C_6H_{12}O_6$ -> $2C_2H_5OH + 2CO_2$

Applications:
- **carbon neutral biofuel/petrol**
- drinks
- solvent for polar, non-polar & ionic compounds
- plastics
- dyes

Carbon neutral: an activity that has no net annual carbon emissions to the atmosphere (greenhouse gas).
-> the CO_2 released when burning the biofuel was removed by plants during growth (does not include CO_2 from farm machinery or making fertilizer)

Polymers

Definition; Polymer reaction equation; Rules for equation; Characteristics of reaction; List of polymers with applications; Characteristics; Disposing

Polymers

Long chain molecules of monomers *(poly – many)*

Propene	poly(propene)
Monomer	Repeating unit / Repeat unit

Rules
- draw square bracket through middle of bond
- polymer chain is built only from carbons with a double bond, **all other carbons form side chains**
- remember to put '**n**' on both sides of equation

Reaction characteristics
- **addition polymerization**
- 100 % atom economy (no waste products)
- Peroxide initiators (high temperature / pressure)
- Radical mechanism

Name from monomer
Polyethene – cheap, strong, moulded => bags, bottles, bowls
Polypropene – strong fibers, high elasticity => crates, robes, carpets
Polystyrene – cheap, moulded, foam => outer cases, packaging
Polytetrafluoroethene (Teflon) - inert, non-stick -> coating for frying pans
PVC (polyvinyl chloride) – waterproof, hard, flexible => sheets, wire
insulation, records

Characteristics
- Not biodegradable
- Unreactive because they are saturated alkanes
- London forces between polymer chains determine melting point

Disposing
- Landfill
- Burning: toxic gases - HCl neutralized by bases (NaOH) in scrubbers
- Recycling: sorting -> cracking or remoulding -> new plastics

3.5 Alcohols

Alcohols

Three types of alcohols; Characteristics of OH-group;
Dehydration reaction with conditions; Reaction with HX

Alcohols

Propan-1-ol	Propan-2-ol	2-Methyl-propan-2-ol
Primary (1st degree)	Secondary (2nd)	Tertiary (3rd)

-> C with alcohol group is bonded to one, two or three other carbons

Characteristics

- high boiling points (hydrogen bonds)

- C-O bond **polar** (different electronegativities)
  -> **OH** good **leaving group**
  => likes to undergo **elimination & nucleophilic substitution reactions**

Dehydration of alcohol -> Elimination reaction (Condensation)

$$\text{alcohol} \quad -> \quad \text{alkene} \quad + \quad \text{water}$$

Step 1:

Step 2:

Conditions: heating under reflux with H_2SO_{4conc} or H_3PO_4 as catalyst

Formation of Haloalkanes

$$\textbf{R-OH + HX -> R-X + H}_2\textbf{O}$$

-> **Nucleophilic substitution** with halide ions (X^-)

Oxidation of Alcohols
&
Aldehydes/Ketones

Oxidising agent; Oxidation of primary, secondary and tertiary alcohols with equations and conditions; Combustion; Naming aldehydes and ketones; Three tests for aldehydes and ketonse

Oxidation of Alcohols

Oxidising agent
- acidified (H_2SO_4) potassium dichromate:
  orange -> green ($K_2Cr_2O_7 (_{+6})$ -> Cr^{3+})

[O]: oxidising unit (2e⁻ gained)

Primary alcohol + [O] $\overset{\text{distillation, limited}}{\longrightarrow}$ **aldehyde** + H_2O

further oxidation: **aldehyde** + [O] $\overset{\text{reflux, excess}}{\longrightarrow}$ **carboxylic acid**

Primary alcohol + 2[O] $\overset{\text{reflux, excess}}{\longrightarrow}$ **carboxylic acid** + H_2O

Secondary alcohol + [O] $\overset{\text{reflux}}{\longrightarrow}$ **ketone** + H_2O

Tertiary alcohol   ->   does not get oxidised

Burning/Combustion

C_2H_5OH + $3O_2$ -> $2CO_2$ + $3H_2O$

Aldehydes/Ketones

$$H_3C-\overset{\displaystyle O}{\overset{\|}{C}}-CH_3$$

Propanone (propan-2-one)

C=O: carbonyl group

Structural formulae
   CH_3COCH_3

$$H_3C-CH_2-\overset{O}{\underset{H}{C\diagdown}}$$

Propanal

   $CH_3CH_2\textbf{CHO}$
do not write: $CH_3CH_2\textbf{COH}$

Tests to distinguish between Aldehydes and Ketones

Acidified $K_2Cr_2O_7$: orange -> green   (see above)

Tollens: test for aldehydes ($AgNO_3$, ammonia, test tube in warm water bath)
Ag^+ + Aldehyde $_{(+1)}$ -> Carboxylic acid $_{(+3)}$ + **Ag (silver mirror)**

Fehling: test for aldehydes *and sugars* (Cu^{2+}/*tartaric acid*/NaOH, heat)
$2Cu^{2+}$ (blue) + Aldehyde -> $2Cu^+$ + Carboxylic acid (Cu_2O **red** precipitate)

3.6 Organic Analysis

Mass Spectrometry
&
IR Spectroscopy

Applications; Five steps in mass spectrometer; Graph; Rule; Isotope peaks; Molecular ion peak; Function & description of IR spectroscopy; Other applications;

Mass Spectrometry

Applications: measuring relative atomic/molecular masses, identifying organic molecules, control of synthesis, radiocarbon dating (archaeology)

Steps in a Mass spectrometer:
- Vaporisation (heating)
- Ionization (electrospray *or electron gun*)
- Acceleration (electric field) -> same kinetic energy
- TOF: time of flight proportional to mass in drift tube *(or deflection)*
- Detection: ions cause electrical current (electrons flow from detector to positive ion) -> intensity of peak (strength of electrical current) depends on amount of ions (abundance)

=> **Graph:** Relative abundance % (Intensity) / mass-to-charge ratio (m/z)

=> **Only positive ions are detected (always add +-sign to species)**

Isotope peaks: Molecular M+1 peak = C^{13} -> from percentage can calculate number of carbons in molecule: C^{13} 1.1 % one C atom, 2.2 % two C etc.
- Accurate Isotope masses can be used to determine exact relative molecular mass, e.g. compound with Mr = 43.9898 is CO_2 not CH_4 (H = 1.0078, C = 12.0000, O = 15.9949)
- **Do not use Relative Atomic Mass from periodic table for Isotope Mass**

Molecular ion M (peak with largest mass) => Mass of whole molecule

IR spectroscopy

-> To **identify** different types of covalent **bonds** => **functional groups**
-> **Identifying** a **molecule** by comparing pattern of **fingerprint region** (1000 – 1550 cm^{-1}) with known compound

- Absorption of IR radiation lets bond vibrate (different bonds – different frequency)
- Spectrum: transmittance (%) versus wavenumber (cm^{-1})
- transmittance: reverse of absorbance
- wavenumber: inverse of wavelength
- wavenumber: the smaller the less energy
- **check if O-H (alcohol *3400 cm^{-1}* or carboxylic acid *2800 cm^{-1}*) and C=O (carbonyl *1700 cm^{-1}*) peaks are present**
- Data Sheet with functional groups and wavenumbers is provided in exam

Other applications:
- accurate test for alcohol in breath of drunk drivers (evidence in law court)
  -> Ratio of OH-peak to CH peak of Ethanol
- to monitor air pollution (CO_2, NO, SO_2, CH_4)

Separating funnel

Diagram and description

Separating funnel

-> To separate on organic phase from an aqueous phase

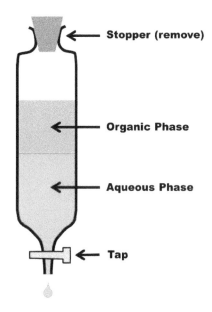

- During the synthesis of an organic compound, in an aqueous solution, the mixture is shaken for a prolonged amount of time in the separating funnel
- Pressure has to be released by opening the stopper frequently (product is volatile)
- Allow the mixture to stand and it will separate into two layers (organic phase & aqueous phase)
- The organic layer is usually on top, due to its lower density
- The aqueous layer contains impurities and can be drained by opening the stopper and the tap
- Close the tap when the organic layer reaches it
- Transfer the organic product into a storage bottle

Reflux apparatus

Diagram and description

Reflux apparatus

-> To heat a reaction mixture with volatile liquids

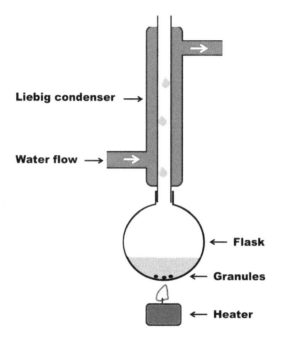

- Most organic reactions need heating for the reaction to happen
- Volatile reactants or products would evaporate and escape as gases
- The flask cannot be closed otherwise it would explode
- To prevent evaporation the gaseous compounds are condensed back into liquids, in the Liebig condenser
- These liquids drop back into the reaction flask
- Here they are collected (products) or continue to react (reactants)
- Anti-bumping granules smooth the boiling process

Distillation Apparatus
&
Drying with Anhydrous Salts

Diagram and description:
Description of drying with anhydrous salts;

Distillation apparatus

-> To separate different fractions of a mixture by boiling points

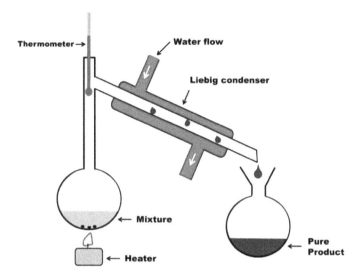

- After an organic reaction there is usually a mixture of products and unreacted reactants
- The desired product can be separated from the mixture at its boiling point by heating
- Compounds with lower boiling points evaporate first
- They condense in the Liebig-cooler and are collected
- The collection vessel is changed when the boiling point of the desired product is reached (indicated by the thermometer: the temperature remains constant for a while)
- This pure product is then collected and stored
- If the product still contains impurities it can be distilled again

Drying with Anhydrous Salts

-> anhydrous salts are used to remove traces of water from an organic product

- After separation of an organic product from the reaction mixture, with a separating funnel or distillation, it might still contain traces of water
- These traces can be removed by adding solid anhydrous salts like $MgSO_4$ or $CaCl_2$
- The water gets incorporated into the salt as water of crystallization
- The salt is then removed by filtration or decanting

The Periodic Table of Elements

(1)	(2)											(13)	(14)	(15)	(16)	7	0 (8)
1	2	3	4	5	6	7							4	5	6	(17)	(18)
							1.0 **H** hydrogen 1										4.0 **He** helium 2
6.9 **Li** lithium 3	9.0 **Be** beryllium 4											10.8 **B** boron 5	12.0 **C** carbon 6	14.0 **N** nitrogen 7	16.0 **O** oxygen 8	19.0 **F** fluorine 9	20.2 **Ne** neon 10
23.0 **Na** sodium 11	24.3 **Mg** magnesium 12	(3)	(4)	(5)	(6)	(7)	(8)	(9)	(10)	(11)	(12)	27.0 **Al** aluminium 13	28.1 **Si** silicon 14	31.0 **P** phosphorus 15	32.1 **S** sulfur 16	35.5 **Cl** chlorine 17	39.9 **Ar** argon 18
39.1 **K** potassium 19	40.1 **Ca** calcium 20	45.0 **Sc** scandium 21	47.9 **Ti** titanium 22	50.9 **V** vanadium 23	52.0 **Cr** chromium 24	54.9 **Mn** manganese 25	55.8 **Fe** iron 26	58.9 **Co** cobalt 27	58.7 **Ni** nickel 28	63.5 **Cu** copper 29	65.4 **Zn** zinc 30	69.7 **Ga** gallium 31	72.6 **Ge** germanium 32	74.9 **As** arsenic 33	79.0 **Se** selenium 34	79.9 **Br** bromine 35	83.8 **Kr** krypton 36
85.5 **Rb** rubidium 37	87.6 **Sr** strontium 38	88.9 **Y** yttrium 39	91.2 **Zr** zirconium 40	92.9 **Nb** niobium 41	95.9 **Mo** molybdenum 42	[98] **Tc** technetium 43	101.1 **Ru** ruthenium 44	102.9 **Rh** rhodium 45	106.4 **Pd** palladium 46	107.9 **Ag** silver 47	112.4 **Cd** cadmium 48	114.8 **In** indium 49	118.7 **Sn** tin 50	121.8 **Sb** antimony 51	127.6 **Te** tellurium 52	126.9 **I** iodine 53	131.3 **Xe** xenon 54
132.9 **Cs** caesium 55	137.3 **Ba** barium 56	138.9 **La*** lanthanum 57	178.5 **Hf** hafnium 72	180.9 **Ta** tantalum 73	183.8 **W** tungsten 74	186.2 **Re** rhenium 75	190.2 **Os** osmium 76	192.2 **Ir** iridium 77	195.1 **Pt** platinum 78	197.0 **Au** gold 79	200.6 **Hg** mercury 80	204.4 **Tl** thallium 81	207.2 **Pb** lead 82	209.0 **Bi** bismuth 83	[209] **Po** polonium 84	[210] **At** astatine 85	[222] **Rn** radon 86
[223] **Fr** francium 87	[226] **Ra** radium 88	[227] **Ac*** actinium 89	[261] **Rf** rutherfordium 104	[262] **Db** dubnium 105	[266] **Sg** seaborgium 106	[264] **Bh** bohrium 107	[277] **Hs** hassium 108	[268] **Mt** meitnerium 109	[271] **Ds** darmstadtium 110	[272] **Rg** roentgenium 111							

* Lanthanide series

140 **Ce** cerium 58	141 **Pr** praseodymium 59	144 **Nd** neodymium 60	[147] **Pm** promethium 61	150 **Sm** samarium 62	152 **Eu** europium 63	157 **Gd** gadolinium 64	159 **Tb** terbium 65	163 **Dy** dysprosium 66	165 **Ho** holmium 67	167 **Er** erbium 68	169 **Tm** thulium 69	173 **Yb** ytterbium 70	175 **Lu** lutetium 71

* Actinide series

232 **Th** thorium 90	[231] **Pa** protactinium 91	238 **U** uranium 92	[237] **Np** neptunium 93	[242] **Pu** plutonium 94	[243] **Am** americium 95	[247] **Cm** curium 96	[245] **Bk** berkelium 97	[251] **Cf** californium 98	[254] **Es** einsteinium 99	[253] **Fm** fermium 100	[256] **Md** mendelevium 101	[254] **No** nobelium 102	[257] **Lr** lawrencium 103

CPSIA information can be obtained
at www.ICGtesting.com
Printed in the USA
BVHW06s0530010518
514824BV00033B/1031/P